ROBERT MAASS

LITTLE TRUCKS
WITH
BIG JOBS

HENRY HOLT AND COMPANY

NEW YORK

PLANE TUG

Big trucks have big jobs, moving everything imaginable across town and country.

But there are smaller trucks that also have big jobs. An airplane must be pushed out from the gate before starting its engines. This is done by a truck called a plane tug.

STREET SWEEPER

City streets are kept clean
by the swirling brooms
of a street sweeper.

TELEPHONE TRUCK

Sometimes extra pay phones are
needed at an outdoor event or when
telephone service is interrupted.
A telephone truck provides
a connection.

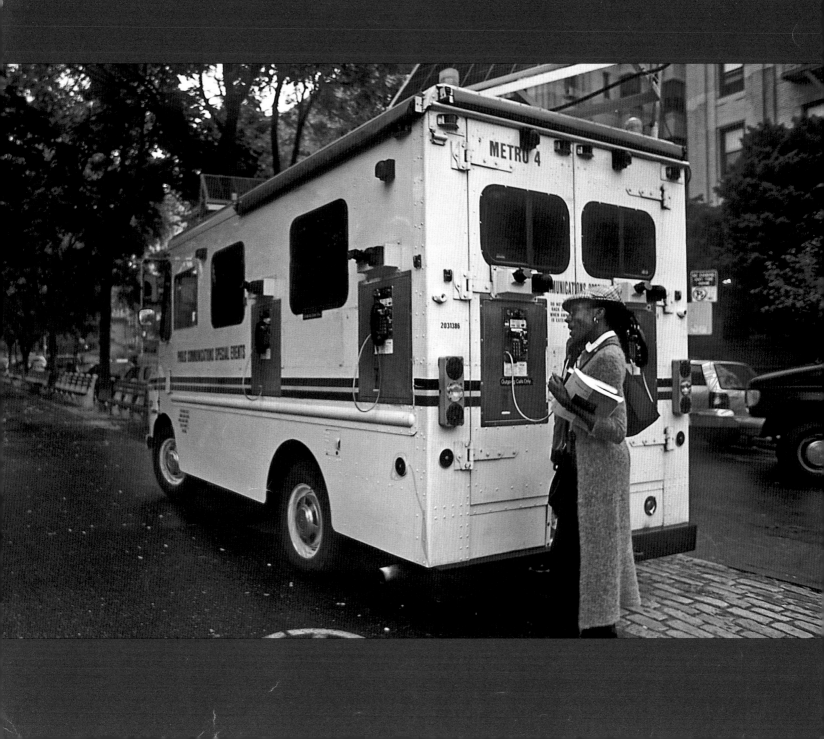

GARBAGE TRUCK

A big garbage truck takes
away household garbage
while a smaller garbage truck
can fit in tight spots like the
winding sidewalks of a park.

FORKLIFT

A forklift can lift a heavy load
many times its weight.
It is often used to
unload bigger
trucks.

ZAMBONI

When the ice rink needs smoothing,
bring in a Zamboni!

CABLE TRUCK

How do you get telephone, cable, and Internet service? A cable truck lays the wires underground that will make the connections.

PICKUP TRUCK

A pickup truck can do so many things, from hauling material in its bed to pulling big loads behind.

MAIL TRUCK

Whether you live in town or in the country, the mail truck keeps you in touch with the world.

AMBULANCE

No truck is more important than an ambulance. This truck transports people who need medical care to a hospital.

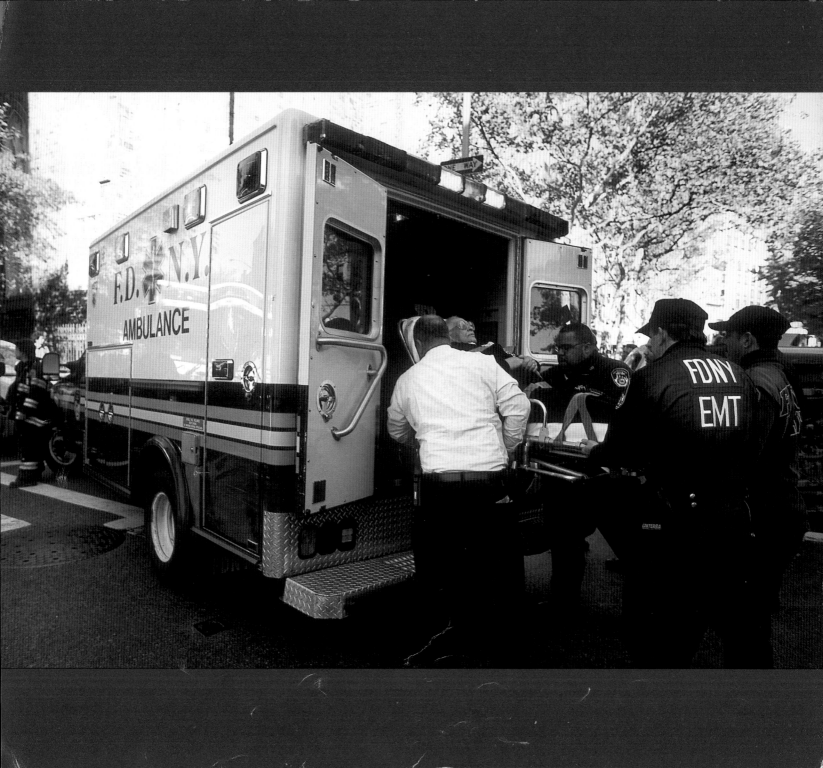

PRODUCE TRUCK

A produce truck brings
fresh fruits and vegetables
to the neighborhood.

CAMPER

Some folks camp in tents while others use a camper truck, where they can feel at home on the road.

TOW TRUCK

When a car breaks down or has
an accident, it is hauled away
by a powerful tow truck.

GLASS TRUCK

A glass truck carries all
sizes of glass, tightly tied
to special holders, so the glass
won't break on the way
to its destination.

ICE CREAM TRUCK

Nothing could be more
welcoming than the ringing
bells of an ice cream
truck on a
hot summer
evening.

Dedicated
to hard-working
drivers of little
(and big) trucks
everywhere

Henry Holt and Company, LLC, *Publishers since 1866*
175 Fifth Avenue, New York, New York 10010
www.henryholtchildrensbooks.com

Henry Holt® is a registered trademark of Henry Holt and Company, LLC.
Copyright © 2007 by Robert Maass
All rights reserved.
Distributed in Canada by H. B. Fenn and Company Ltd.

Library of Congress Cataloging-in-Publication Data
Maass, Robert. Little trucks with big jobs / Robert Maass.—1st ed.
p. cm.
ISBN-13: 978-0-8050-7748-3 / ISBN-10: 0-8050-7748-0
1. Trucks—Juvenile literature. I. Title.
TL230.15.M328 2007   629.224—dc22   2006030617

First Edition—2007 / Designed by Meredith Pratt
Printed in the United States of America on acid-free paper. ∞

1 3 5 7 9 10 8 6 4 2

These photographs were produced on conventional film and digitally.